PITCH

How To Give An Elevator Pitch For Tech Start-Ups

DAN GUDEMA

How To Give An Elevator Pitch For Tech Start-Ups
Copyright © 2015, 2016 by Dan Gudema

All rights reserved. No part of this book may be reproduced or transmitted in any form or by any means without written permission from the author.

ISBN-10: 1505318572

ISBN-13: 978-1505318579

DEDICATION

This book is dedicated to those we left behind, who did not make it this far, Scott Wheeler, Katie Pantoine, Regan Bond.

Contents

INTRODUCTION	9
YOUR CONTENT	23
CRITICAL TARGETS	31
SECONDARY TARGETS	43
STORY ELEMENTS FOR ELEVATOR PITCHES	53
START BIG AND END BIG	63
BELIEVABILITY	71
ANSWERING QUESTIONS	79
WHAT NOT TO DO	87
FOLLOWING UP WITH INVESTORS	101
YOUR CHECKLIST	109
NOTES	113
A FEW FINAL WORDS	123
QUOTED PEOPLE	125
YOUR READING LIST	127
ABOUT THE AUTHOR	129

ACKNOWLEDGMENTS

Thank you to Marc Wigder John Kemp and all who believed in our vision at The Greenhouse. Thank you to Adam Kravitz Terry Aronson, Brandon Esposito, Alan Shimmel and Aramas Kaloustian for being gracious panel members. Thank you to Mark Laymon for building a new tech community in Boca Raton. Special thanks to a truly excellent Florida Atlantic University MBA communication program. Thank you to Tom, Donna, Norman, Madeline, Victor and Max for having to listen to me talk about writing books. Finally thank you to my wife Linda for taking time to edit my manuscript.

*INVESTORS DON'T INVEST IN THE HORSE;
THEY INVEST IN THE JOCKEY*

Introduction

You are waiting to get up and pitch your tech start-up in front of a crowd of investors!

You are next in line. Finally they call your name.

You get a little nervous, but are determined to do the best job you can.

You stand up.

You start your three minute elevator pitch. When it ends, the shark tank asks you questions. You do your best to answer those questions. When it is all said and done, you really don't know how well you did.

The fantasy result would be that somebody totally got it and wants to invest in it. Quite often, it ends without any interest. But next time won't be the same, because you will be prepared by reading this book!

Have you have sent in an application or agreed to

give a three minute tech start-up pitch at a local start-up pitch event to raise capital for your tech venture?

You are either the founder or a partner in the venture. You may have your technology already developed or you may have an idea on a napkin.

Standing and delivering everything necessary an investor needs to know in three minutes is not for the faint of heart.

It is difficult!

It makes us nervous!

You will lose your train of thought!

You will lose your mind! We have had people run off stage in fear at our events. It is easier to present to 600 people or 60,000 people than to 30 or up to 100 peers in a room. It may be just you and one investor at a networking meeting.

You need to be prepared.

You need to be able to get across everything necessary in less than three minutes or even two minutes. Or the dreaded one minute pitch!

You need to concisely let the investor know what you are doing and what you are looking for. Can you do it? If not, you need to work on this pitch, over and over. That is why you are reading this book! You need to get educated on what needs to be in the pitch and what works and what does not work. You need to perfect your three minute tech start-up pitch to get that seed capital!

Who should read this book?

This book is primarily for tech start-ups getting ready to do an elevator pitch to raise capital. However, even if you are not raising capital, you need to be able to explain your tech venture in less than three minutes to anybody. This book is for a tech entrepreneur who is trying to explain why they need capital for their start-up. We use the word tech start-ups very generously here. No matter what business you are going into these days, there is almost certainly a connection with technology. Even if you are opening up a chicken ranch, you need to have some technology advantage to compete.

If you are booked for a pitch event tomorrow night,

then buy this book as a Kindle eBook now and read it this evening! This book is also great for undergraduate and MBA classes who are getting ready to compete in a business plan or pitch contest. If you are an angel, a venture capitalist, a serial entrepreneur or just interested in the subject, you will get something out of this book. If you have a general interest in tech start-ups and business concepts, this book will be very useful. You don't have to be giving a tech start-up pitch to get something out of this book. You can be getting ready for your future pitch. Or you can be preparing to coach someone else! If you work for a company, school non-profit or other entity selling your idea is critical. The skill of explaining your idea to decision-makers or customers of any kind will make things happen.

How does is a three minute tech start-up pitch differ from a ten page pitch deck?

Well, for one, a ten page pitch deck requires a Power Point deck, Google Presentation or Prezi and a screen to project your pitch deck on. For a three minute tech start-up pitch, you may have the luxury of one page on the screen introducing you, saying your company name, logo, tagline (if you have one), and some contact info. Maybe it can have your social media links. Quite often you are asked to give a pitch on the spot to an investor with no Power Point or notes. The ten page pitch deck is a standard in the industry, but it is not accomplished in less than ten minutes. That is why we have used a three minute tech start-up pitch to give potential investors a taste of what you are working on. There is also a dreaded one minute tech start-up pitch. It is practically impossible to perfect. The one minute pitch has been used by The Funding Post, a national event company that arranges for angels and venture capitalists to speak and become familiar with current trends. They also let you pitch to angels and venture capital at their events. I don't recommend the one minute tech start-up pitch. It is quite useless. Three or two minutes is enough to get all the points across about what you do.

Why Did I Write This Book?

In 2014 we began running tech start-up pitch events in South Florida. What I found was the people who are attempting to create tech start-ups are quite often terrible at pitching their ideas. I know, I am one of them. I have done a bunch of pitches to raise capital over the past couple years as well. I had one pitch, where they asked the audience "who understood what Dan was actually talking about." Only 20% raised their hands. This is not good! So when I started to run our tech start-up pitch events, I quickly realized that we needed a pitch training class. That class ended up being a great way to find out if there was demand to understand how to do this three minute pitch. It was about how to change from a completely off the cuff, ill-prepared start-up pitch to a succinct and understandable version of your pitch that makes sense and can get you the next step, a meeting with an investor.

What we told the students in our pitch training class is that they need to hit what I call 'critical targets' in the three minute pitch. They also needed to become actors on the stage. In a lot of ways, a tech pitch is a drama. Investors need to understand right away what the pitch is about, why they are listening and what this start-up pitch person is seeking. There needs to be a clear succinct message and a reason for the investor to want to learn more! How you present yourself is critical to success in pitching your venture. How you are perceived is critical. Luckily we can change the perception of investors who are listening to your pitch. None of us are perfect. The question is do you want to take the time to fix your pitch. You need to put your time into preparing for your pitch. You need to repeat it over and over until you have it down cold. In the end you will appear to be a natural at giving your tech start-up pitch. Great tech pitchers will never tell you about the level of preparation involved. Do not underestimate the time involved in getting ready to pitch.

2016 Update

This book is an update of the original "How To Give An Elevator Pitch For Tech Start-Ups" that I wrote in early 2015. Since writing this book we have run another 7 events, or one every 3 months for the past year and a half. In this 2nd edition, we added questions to each chapter to make the book more of an interactive experience. You need to take time and fill in all these questions that you are being asked at the end of each chapter. This interaction may be just what you need to get ready for your pitch event. Please enjoy the book, and let me know if you have any feedback at dan@startuppop.com. Good luck at your pitch, tonight!

A Little History Of The Three Minute Elevator Pitch

There has been some speculation that one of the robber barons would let people into their private elevator on the way to their office perhaps on Wall Street. They had one to three minutes to get the summary of their business proposition across. At least this myth sounds good. The actual people an elevator pitch has been attributed to, according to Wikipedia (as you know the on again/off again source of all reliable information) is Ilene Rosenzweig and Michael Caruso (while he was Editor for Vanity Fair). They would give people just enough time in the elevator to get their point across. If they liked what they heard, they'd give out them a business card, to theoretically set up another meeting. That is how the word elevator got into the saying "elevator pitch." We specifically focus on three minutes, because it is much better than one or two minutes and a lot better than having to listen to a ten page Power Point pitch. If the time is used carefully, it can make all the difference for investors to evaluate if they need to have the next discussion.

Next Steps

If investors have an interest in a tech start-up at a tech start-up pitch event, they will typically ask for one of two things right away; an executive summary or a pitch deck. You should naturally have these ready to go in your arsenal. We refer to these documents as **Tools For Your Tech Start-Up**. The three minute elevator pitch is one of six major tools you need to have ready for investors, partners, employees, advisers, mentors, customers and other interested parties. As you master these tools you will have everything you need to confidently present your ideas in a way that will get you funded.

Though out this book, there will be sections that are added to allow you to work out your own 3 minute elevator pitch. If this is the printed version, take out a pen and answer these questions the best you can.

What is the name of your company?

_____

_____

_____

Describe your business?

_____

_____

_____

Why are you pitching? (What are you looking for?)

_____

_____

Where are you at with product development?

_____

_____

ANYBODY CAN MAKE THINGS COMPLICATED, VERY FEW CAN MAKE IT SIMPLE!

JOHN KEMP

Your Content

The first thing we learned when running the very first three minute elevator pitch training class for tech start-ups is most tech entrepreneurs had a difficult time explaining what they were doing.

You need to be able to boil what you do down to one sentence. It is very important to get this concise. The shorter, the better. A lot of tech entrepreneurs think that laying on a pile of techno-garble or throwing around a lot of data and complexity will impress the potential investor. Not so. One of my mentors, John Kemp, says "Anybody can make things complicated, very few can make it simple!"

Get All Your Information Together

What I recommend is that you have to take all of the information about your product and write the important technical features and descriptive information. You can either use paper or 3x5 cards. Here is an example for a made up app called "Lawn Mower Timer".

- Determines when to mow the lawn.
- Is a mobile app.
- Has an automated calendar feature.
- Has a free version.
- Has a paid version.
- Has a built in email reminder it sends you.
- Has a built in Text Message reminder it sends you.
- Can schedule your next lawn mowing appointment.

Then take each one and order them by what is most important. For instance, it may be more important that you let people know it is a mobile app. You need to order them in importance from the mind of the investor. You also need to determine what is important enough for investors to know versus stuff that they would not care about from a product standpoint.

The Tagline

A tagline is either one sentence or a few short words that describes what you do. From all these product/service features you could put together a tagline like:

> Lawn Mower Timer is a mobile app based lawn reminder solution with a free and paid version that schedules a lawn person to cut your lawn.

Notice how I left out some of the minor points. The email and text message reminders are cool, but they don't have to be in your tagline. You can add another sentence to the first one like:

> Lawn Mower Timer is a mobile app based lawn reminder solution with a free and paid version that schedules a lawn person to cut your lawn. Lawn Mower Timer will send out reminders by email and text message that will precisely let you know when your lawn must be cut.

The end result is the investors now know what you are building, that there is a paid version and what kind of features it offers.

Finding A Red Herring

Sometimes entrepreneurs fail to understand how important a specific aspect of their pitch can be. The right piece of information can impact the mind of an investor. For instance, expertise or current success in the field is terrific. One of the students in my pitch class held up a product and announced to us that he had already sold 100. I looked at him and said, "Wow, you need to start with that."

Attention Getter: "**You Should Start With That!**"

Later on in this book, we will talk about starting big and ending big. What we mean by "Start With That" is highlighting overwhelmingly important that will be an attention getter. One of my students for instance was developing a new kind of Hookah, with some new kind of technology. When he mentioned that he had worked for NASA in the past as an aerospace engineer, I found that fascinating. I knew investors would eat that up. He had to start with that. Don't hide this critical information that can set you apart, use it to your advantage.

What is your company tagline?

_____

_____

_____

_____

Who is on the management team?

_____

_____

_____

_____

What are you realistically looking to get pitching?

_____

_____

_____

_____

THE MOST ATTRACTIVE THING YOU CAN EVER SAY TO AN ANGEL INVESTOR IS "I AM NOT LOOKING FOR CAPITAL."

Critical Targets

I like to use the words "critical targets" to describe your path to success. Your mission is to deliver these critical targets in three minutes. For those who have not given a three minute elevator pitch, be aware that it may sound simple. It is not. You can easily make a few big mistakes and really send the wrong message or no message at all! I know. I have done this. These critical targets are the things you must hit like an airplane bomber in the military. If you miss these targets your investors will be both confused and generally put off. You only get one chance with most investors. Hitting critical targets is a way to know you are making sure you are getting your points across. Here is a list of these critical targets.

1) Say Your Name, Company, and Product. Describe Your Start-Up

2) What Is Your Financial Model? (How You Get Paid)

3) What Is The Total Market Opportunity "$" And Describe Your Customer?

4) How Are You Getting To Market? (Go To Market Strategy)

5) What Are You Looking For? (Investors? Partners? Technology? Advisors?)

It is important to understand, from a business perspective, that the product is no more important than the other critical targets. Notice that the product description is only one of 5 critical targets. That means that you could spend only 20% of the pitch on the actual product or service and you would be fine. This is not a fixed rule. You can throw all these rules out the window and use your own rules. As long as you hit the critical targets you are good!

But once again, the product or service is only one of 5 critical targets. This is an important point for start-up entrepreneurs. The lesson is that the other 80% needs to be expounded upon or you will not be taken seriously.

Say Your Name and Your Company Name

Remember to say your name and your company name. You would not believe it, but people forget these things. One of the things that happens when we get up in front of people is we get nervous. We get so wrapped up in describing the product that we forget the critical targets, lose our minds and miss our critical targets. Of course you would not forget your name or company! Trust me, I have.

What Is Your Financial Model?

Believe or not a lot of tech start-ups get hung up on this simple question. If you can't or won't answer it, you should stop or rethink your venture now! It is not a mystery. It is not an afterthought. It needs to be clear. It can change, but you need to put a stake in the ground now.

Is this a product for sale? Is this a recurring online monthly payment solution. Is it a one-time payment? Do you get paid when a lead converts? Do you get paid as part of a partnership deal? Do you finally make the money when the venture or technology gets acquired by a larger corporation. That is a valid business model. It is a very weak business model compared with all the other business models, but who knows, some investors may go for it. I wouldn't if I was investing.

What Is Your Total Acquirable Market (TAM) Opportunity?

The TAM for your start-up refers to a realistic market share capture number from a financial perspective. It can be monthly, yearly or over three years. So let's say the entire dating business is $2 billion a year in sales. And you have come to the conclusion that the most you can possibly capture of that amount is 1%, because you are building for a limited segment of the market. The realistic TAM may actually be lower, but 1% would be equal to $20 million a year. That is the real opportunity or TAM, not $2 billion. Investors want to know this number, not pie in the sky numbers.

This can be a guess, but it can also be a highly researched answer, backed by data and valid assumptions. You can easily find information on the internet that says the entire market value of an industry. We will look at the TAM opportunity for both our made up Lawn Mower Timer app and a dating mobile app.

You need to come up with a theoretical calculation that gives you an answer to what is the total market opportunity. If you cannot easily find a number in some online article, you need to extrapolate and derive a number, preferably a monthly or yearly revenue number. If an investor asks you how you came up with that number, give him the derivation calculation.

So let's say you are building a new dating app and you want to say you are going to capture 1% of the market. Well there is data out there saying that $2 billion is spent yearly on online dating. And if you were to capture 1% of the market, or what we refer to as TAM (Total Addressable Market), you would then be able to capture $20 Million a year in sales.

For my mowing company, we may not be able to find this total market size anywhere online so we can figure out how many houses are in the US.

Let's say there are 50 million homes with lawns. And let's say that each lawn costs $20 to cut a month. Let's use a 6 month cycle. So, we would end up with $20 x 50 million x 6 months. The end result is that there is about a $6 billion dollar total market a year for cutting lawns. Not too shabby. Sounds a lot better than the online dating industry! You claim to want to capture 1% of this market. You would end up with a $60 million dollar yearly opportunity. When you state your market opportunity is $60 million a year, you are not just making this stuff up. You are backing it up with your calculations and now some confidence. Finally your customers are home owners. So it is understandable who they are and what they need.

The home owners need their lawn cut!

How Are You Getting To Market?

With our techie/engineering minds, we sometimes overlook that there needs to be a way to get our product or service to market. Will we make a great product that nobody knows about and no one will ever find out about? Having a plan on getting to market is very important! This is critical in your elevator pitch. Quite possibly you may have several ways of getting to market. That's ok. Let's say this lawn cutting app can be used to schedule a lawn to be cut. Let's say you are going to market through Google Pay Per Click and Print Ads in local magazines. The point here is you have a plan to get to market. Probably just as important is the investor sees you have done some basic research and have come up with a strategy.

One thing an elevator pitch can show is that you have some brains and have put some time and energy you have put into your idea. You have to show that you have passion.

What Do You Want?

This sounds very straight-forward. However, this

can be a bit of a trick question. Many tech start-ups are looking for seed capital. Do you really need it? You have to ask yourself this question. Sometimes it is best to stay away from the words 'looking for capital'. You can always start with 'looking for advisers, mentors, partners'. You can also mention that you are looking for a technology partner, programmer or a business person to partner with. It is not a straight-forward as saying you are looking for money. In fact, you should pretty much stay away from the word money. It is more appropriate to say capital. If you are looking for the first capital investment, then it is seed capital. If you are looking for a second round of capital investment, then you say a second round or a Series A if it is a public offering. You need to be as specific as possible. The investors know what level they are seeking. If you are already in revenue and are past a seed round of capital, you may be exactly what they have been seeking.

Complete Your Mission!

It is often a nerve wracking experience for many to get up and pitch for capital. Even though we may not like to do it, we should push ourselves to do it regardless of what we like. Pitching for capital is a tried and true method to get noticed. And you have to be in it to win it. Remember the critical targets. Hit those targets. Hit those targets even if you are not funny, are extremely nervous, about to throw up and are not the best speaker or are not prepared for the pitch. Hitting the targets is key to get your point across.

We will cover the intangibles of a three minute elevator pitch for tech start-ups in the next couple of chapters.

Describe your product or service you provide?

_____

_____

_____

What is your financial "business" model?

_____

_____

_____

What is the total marketing opportunity? $$

_____

_____

Your go to market strategy?

_____

_____

WHEN THEY SAY ASK YOUR FRIENDS AND FAMILY TO BE YOUR EARLY INVESTORS, THEY DON'T REALLY MEAN YOUR FRIENDS AND FAMILY!

JACK KARABEES

Secondary Targets

After reviewing the critical targets, there are a lot of other potential add-ons for your pitch.

Before we get to Start Big and End Big later in this book, we have to find those unique value propositions you bring to the show and get them out on the proverbial table. These are the amazingly important elements you need in your pitch to make you stand out immediately from the pack.

How Do We Find These Hidden Gems?

First off, let's not be coy about it. There are things that make YOU very special! You are going to see a list of secondary targets on the next page. They may or may not fit who you are. Find one that makes sense.

You being different or special is important. The more it relates to your start-up tech pitch, the better. It could be your major in college. It could be that you spent time working for the Rothchild wine family in Dijon in the south of France. You may have worked for a senator on Capitol Hill. I did. You may have played triple A baseball or been an artist living in Amsterdam. It should relate at least to your life and it should relate to your start-up.

Let's find out what makes you special. For instance, when one of our entrepreneurs mentioned to us that he spent time as an engineer at NASA, this is not something to be ignored. I worked with a kid who just graduated from the Stanford computer science program. That is important! I wrote a blog article about finding that unique thing that people will find irresistible and not turn their attention away from.

Marketers will this your 'story'. I call this your shtick.

What Is Your Shtick?

Shtick, which means "gimmick" in Yiddish, refers to your signature behavior, in a Catskills comedian kind of way.

To me, it's why people remember you. It can be most anything, but quite often it is what you have already accomplished. For instance, I had built up the largest speed dating company, Pre-Dating.com, in the US with a partner. We grew to over 100 cities and sold the company to Cupid.com 2004. For whatever reason, when I mention this at networking events, I get their attention.

Your hidden gem is an attention getter. Problem is, sometimes people giving a pitch have a shtick which is negative.

What is important is not what you think. It is important what the investors think. For instance, having a billionaire father is always a positive. Having a previous successful business is a great point to mention. Being trained at MIT, Harvard or Stanford is instant credibility. Now, we know that going to these schools ultimately is not really credibility in terms of running a start-up, but we are interested in what will turn on investors. They will listen up.

So, what is your hidden gem?

A List of Potential Shticks

1. Your Entire Work History.
2. A Specific Company You worked for.
3. Your Parents.
4. Your Hobby.
5. Your Interest.
6. Your Religion.
7. Your School You Attended.
8. Your School Project You Created.
9. Who You Worked With In The Past.
10. The Person Who Influenced You. (Depends if this is your brother or Guy Kawasaki).
11. Something Funny
12. Something Honest
13. Something Personal (Telling a personal story)
14. Your last business!
15. What you failed at, and what you learned!

Your shtick is not the same thing as a secondary target. Secondary targets are things we need to hit with a bow and arrow.

Secondary Targets

Here is a list of the secondary targets you may try to hit along the way. They include:

The Management Team
Competitive Analysis
Competitive Advantage
Financial Analysis
Three Year Pro Forma Net Income
Exit Strategy
Partnerships
Trends
Advisory Board Members

I could probably come up with a dozen other secondary targets. If you are very familiar with a start-up tech pitch deck, you will have seen these slides in your deck. They are typically slides you put together for the bigger presentation. For the elevator pitch, it is a little different. You don't have time for these items. Generally speaking don't use them, unless you have an over-riding reason to. There are no rules to this game. You need to make the rules. If you are targeting funding a $140 million dollar revenue a month business, let them know that. You have the critical targets you need to cover. Then you have the stuff that gets attention, but it quite often is the secondary stuff.

Remove All Unnecessary Items

Take all these extra pieces of information and put them down on paper. Then you need to sort them by what is attention getting and critical. From this list, you can remove things from the bottom of the list. I mentioned the management team. Just because you have a management team does not mean mentioning it or rattling off all their names during your elevator pitch, especially if nothing stands out. If you are 5 white kids from the suburbs with average names and nothing extraordinary, maybe you should just hold back on mentioning them. When you say that John Scully or Mark Zuckerberg is on your team or board, now that's a different story.

What is your shtick?
_____
_____
_____
_____

What is your competitive advantage?
_____
_____
_____

How/when do you get the investor's money back?
_____
_____
_____

*GOOD STORIES ARE ABOUT THE MOMENT
WHEN SOMEBODY'S LIFE CHANGES.*

DUBA LEIBELL

Story Elements for Elevator Pitches

In the early nineties I was determined to be a screenwriter. I enrolled at the New School in the West Village in New York City and studied with the writer of Gunsmoke and Hart to Hart. It was a hardcore screen writing class. I loved it. It was a breath of fresh air compared with my engineering job at Bell Atlantic Mobile (aka Verizon Wireless). I even liked it better when I worked on other people's spec scripts.

When I moved to South Florida, I studied screenwriting with a group of writers with a well-known writer, Duba Leibell, in Miami Beach for years. I spent a lot more time editing other people's scripts. I found working with these writers, trying to get their story in good shape, similar to building a software program. I found there was a relationship between programming and story development. They both require as much planning as actual work. The better the plan or architecture the better the final product.

What attracted me to screen writing was story development. I have always known there is a relationship between business presentations and story-telling. The question I have always wanted to figure out is how to use story development to effectively present one's ideas.

We all know stories have a beginning, middle and end. They all tend to try to make a point or accomplish getting across something that needs to be told with purpose. A good story always seems to reach a level of completion for the reader or listener. A good story can make us feel great. A poorly told story can confuse an audience.

In creating your elevator pitch, you need to think of your pitch as a story.

Does your pitch lend itself to story elements? Was there a saga and interesting story about how you got started in this business. The elements required for a good story are as old as

Dan's Dos & Don'ts

DON'T ramble on and on.

A good pitch is short, simple, and very, very specific. Aim for a two minute version of your pitch that nicely and succinctly conveys the bones of your business model, and your shtick which is your "unfair advantage."

*Of course also include an **exact** funding target.*

You'll do better by not trying to raise "between $1.5 – 2 million." You're raising "$1.8 million."

human history and are a factor in what drives the human race.

Setting The Stage

Your pitch can start with setting the stage. Throw out a few items, statistics or information about your business. This can take the form of "Did you know that this year more than 30,000 people will die from lung cancer?" or "Every month over 500 million emails or texts are sent out to people saying can you send me your address?" I tend to see data as setting the stage. But it can be most anything, for instance it can be about a place you worked at prior to this start-up.

The Inciting Incident

The next piece we call the inciting incident. For instance, let's say your parent died from lung cancer. If the next words that come out are "that's why I started this business to make sure that other sons do not have to go through what I went through!" That is emotional. It is strong and attention getting. You need to captivate your audience, and this is how to do it. Once again, you need to not forget about your critical targets. You need to weave together your story and the important stuff to make something very unique.

The Turning Point

Some great stories have what we refer to as a turning point. In a screenplay it is when the story hits a critical point and then goes in a completely different direction. In your pitch this could be how you tried to solve this difficult problem and then suddenly you had an "Aha" moment, and figured out what to do. From that point forward you knew that you were on to something big and now you have the prototype right here in your hands.

The Conclusion

One of the minor things we studied in a very good MBA program at Florida Atlantic University is that you need to make sure that in your presentations you don't forget the basics;

Dan's Dos & Don'ts

Do explain:

Why are YOU uniquely qualified to make this business happen?

What gives YOU the advantage over everyone else?

What puts YOUR business above the competitors? (yes there are competitors – and a savvy investor may school you on them!)

Explain the endgame. What's the exit strategy? How /when will the investor get their money back? If it is an acquisition in 3 years' time then give examples of companies that would consider your business an attractive acquisition.

introducing who you are, what you are presenting and at the end thanking the audience for listening. I have forgotten to introduce myself while speaking.

What is important is reinforcing your critical targets to the potential investors.

At the end of the elevator pitch, you should repeat the key points of the pitch. If you need to emphasize something in particular, then hit that target in one final sentence like "Our product x is going to sell to a market of 125 million global organizations, with a potential of $120 million a month in recurring monthly sales. This is a unique product that is not like anything else on the market and we are going to be live with our first beta version in January." I am just throwing out a few words here. I hope you get the point.

Tell me the story of how you got started.

_____

_____

_____

_____

What was that inciting incident that made you say ah-ha I am going to do this startup?

_____

_____

_____

What event, milestone, person you met, partner, trend or other thing has happened so far?

_____

_____

_____

HURRYDATE WAS 3 MINUTES, PRE-DATING WAS 6 MINUTES, 8MINUTEDATING WAS 8 MINUTES, BUT I NEEDED 20 MINUTES. SO I MET NOBODY!

*DAN GUDEMA
ON TRYING TO MEET
A WOMAN SPEED
DATING*

Start Big And End Big

Let's back up a second and consider some items we have discussed so far, like creating the story, hitting the critical targets and other small factors.

Great pitches don't just have a cadence to them, they start big and end big.

If you can add this to your elevator pitch, it will serve two purposes. The first is you will get an investor's attention. The second is to be memorable. So think about how you can get their attention in the beginning. I have seen everything from saying something outrageous, that you can prove, to asking everybody to stand up and stretch. You could say a joke.

Saying Something Funny

Humor sells! Being funny is terrific, especially if it can be part of the overall pitch.

Well, it happens when I was pitching OopsImSingle.com, which never went live, that I wanted to add to the pitch something humorous. In this case, I specifically diverted from the entire presentation right at the beginning and talked about me and my background. I was a bit self-deprecating. That's what makes great humor. I said a joke that explained who I was. I was explaining my background in the dating business, being a partner in Pre-Dating.com, the largest speed dating company in the US. Speed dating was my shtick and gave me some credibility in that market. What I said in the beginning of the pitch was "Hurrydate was 3 minutes, Pre-Dating was 6 minutes, 8MinuteDating was 8 minutes, but I needed 20 minutes, so I met nobody".

If you think this had some serious relevance to the overall pitch, it didn't. But it got a laugh and they got a sense of who I was.

There is something about laughter that is critical to a pitch. It can't all be serious. Well, it can, but if there is room for relevant, ironic humor, it is how you start big and end big.

The End

The final point can be a critical factor in getting a follow-up meeting. You need to find a way to sum it all up and still be memorable. Not sure how you are going to do it, but let's say you should try to have a final point you are making that sets you apart. I heard a pitch in New York City where the ending was simple. He stated "We have made two million dollars in this business already. We are no longer a start-up. If that is what you are looking to invest in. That is who we are". He blew away all the competition!

What is funny about your startup?

_____

_____

_____

Is there a joke in the business or product name?

_____

_____

_____

What amazing fact can you tell me related to this startup? (Like "$500 million people a month email each other and ask for a physical address")

_____

_____

_____

YOU HAVE TO BE BELIEVED TO BE HEARD

BERT DECKER

Believability

I love talking about Bert Decker's "You have to be believed to be heard." I hope from talking about Decker's book, a few people take an interest in Decker and read him. It is a simple theme. The greater the level of believability, the better at getting your point across. When I say believable, it means you are not just trustworthy and say things that are real, it has more to do with really who you are at the core.

You either are a believable person or not. To be believable is to be better understood and be loved! To be loved at the moment you pitch is important. You need it and want it and require it from those listening.

Let's talk a little about believability from a couple different perspectives. How do you become ultimately believable in the short span of less than three minutes? The first, quick answer is be real! By being real, you are who you are. You can try to act like somebody you are not. If you are a technology professional, that is who you are. If you are a salesman, that is who you are. You have to reach in deep and use what you are good at in order to explain what you are doing. This is the thing that makes the most sense. Don't be somebody you are not!

The Tangibles, The Intangibles and Hard Numbers

There are two perspectives to an elevator pitch. Quite frankly if you have a weak business model (or no business model), you are going to be weak from the get go. I am assuming you have considered all the business models and chosen one. See my chapter on Critical Targets. If you have strengthened your business model, and answered all of the Critical Target questions, then believability is the icing on the cake. Trying to just be believable with all weak business answers is something that investors will just see through. There is the fact that being a strong believable person, and getting your point across, will have an impact.

What Can You Do About Believability?

We know appearing passionate and emotional means being perceived as dedication. Your pitch will be stronger. We know that being calmer means being more believable. Listeners do not need to know you are nervous. Everybody gets nervous. I do. What you need to do is mask that nervousness. How do you do this? Once again Decker has a variety of answers. One I remember is to speak slower. If you are nervous take a pause. Speaking with more emphasis and using arm motions helps you seem calmer and believable. It may sound like a trick. It is not. It makes you seem more believable. It is important to take these actions, even if you don't believe in yourself. Having an audience believing in you is the most important part of your pitch.

Getting Stuck

One thing that happens to me when pitching is I find I get stuck. That's why I typically keep a piece of paper with some notes on it to get myself back on track. It's ok to use a prop. I think that makes you very believable. I will look over my notes when I get stuck and find the thing that I needed to get back to discussing with the audience. It is important to make a point right after you get stuck, as though you needed a second to think it through. I believe you can use any problem you run into and use it to your advantage.

What is real and authentic about your pitch?

_____

_____

_____

Why are you so passionate about this idea?

_____

_____

What is something that people love associated with your concept, physical, intangible, emotional?

_____

_____

_____

IF AN INVESTOR HAS NO QUESTIONS EITHER ONE OF FOUR THINGS ARE TRUE; EITHER THEY HAVE NO INTEREST; THEY HAVE A TREMENDOUS INTEREST; THEY JUST WERE NOT LISTENING; OR THEY DIDN'T UNDERSTAND A WORD YOU SAID!

Answering Questions

A lot of pitches end with audience questions. Some do not. If you are in front of a panel or shark tank they will ask you questions in order to find out what you left out of your pitch. Sometimes they let the audience ask questions as well.

Some entrepreneurs are great at answering questions. Some ignore questions they don't want to answer. Sometimes a panel will set you up with a question that you know the answer to on purpose, just to throw you a bone.
Soft Questions And Hard Questions

A lot of people ask questions because there is some critical information you left out of the pitch. If there are no questions then one of several things are true. Either your project is not appropriate for any investors. They just don't have an interest in new types of aquariums. They could be tired as a group and ready to go home. There are ball busters who come to events and spend time criticizing people pitching to whoever is nearby during the event. There are people who ask the toughest questions possible just to get a reaction out of you.

Sometimes really tough questions are asked to figure out whether the venture is really viable. For instance, I heard a pitch for a company that recovered oil wells that filled with water. This company was using a new technology that separates oil from water. I asked one question, "how low does the price of a barrel of oil have to fall for this to be unprofitable?" He answered "under $50 a barrel". This was during the period when prices were over $100 a barrel. Sadly enough this situation occurred within three years. So sometimes an important question is asked.

Anticipating Tough Questions

You may want to anticipate some of the hardest questions that can be asked, especially in one of your vulnerable areas.

I recommend you have a prepared answer for that extra tough question!

FoMO

"fear of missing out"

Fear of missing out or FoMO is "a pervasive apprehension that others might be having rewarding experiences from which one is absent".

Any investor that has been in the game for a while has passed on an opportunity that later went on to be amazingly profitable and successful. And even a newbie investor can feel the pangs of being left out on the next big thing. No one wants to say they COULD HAVE invested early in Apple, Yahoo or the most recent startup that went blue-chip.

Your job is to make them worry they'll regret it if they pass you up.

Be your biggest critic and write down the questions you cannot answer well. Prepare for those questions.

A difficult question is always "what happens if you don't hit your revenue numbers?"

I always answer that we will pivot and succeed in a new direction. I would tell them I have a back-up plan one and back-up plan two. I would answer that we need to be in the market to figure this problem out, but it is not unsolvable.

Great Speakers Solve All Problems

You will notice that people who are naturally great at pitching and selling will always find an answer that is amazingly good. This may seem like natural talent. I think it usually has to do with preparation. The people that are not good at pitching, guess what, they typically did not prepare and winged it. I see a lot of tech people just wing these things.

Think Like An Investor. Be The Devil's Advocate.

In order to prepare for questions, you need to put yourself in the investor seat. You need to be an actor playing the investor part. Even better is having others play this part with you. You probably have a dozen friends and family you can call upon to be the devil's advocate.

What is a real tough question you could be asked? And how do you answer it?

_____

_____

_____

Why are you the guy/gal to do this venture?

_____

_____

_____

Why Now? Why is the timing right for this venture?

_____

_____

_____

YOU CAN HAVE PASSION IN YOUR START-UP PITCH, BUT LEAVE REAL PASSION FOR YOUR SIGNIFICANT OTHER

What Not To Do

So you have gotten this far into my little book about giving elevator pitches and you are close to giving this start-up pitch a try. It could even be this evening. One of the things I did in my elevator pitch training sessions is put together a list of **What Not To Do!** Things not to do are:

- a) Lose Your Mind
- b) Focus Only On Tech
- c) Waste All Of Your Time On Something Not Critical.
- d) Miss A Big Critical Target.
- e) Forget The Thing That Makes You Stand Out (Your Shtick)
- f) Lose Your Mind Again

Let's go through a few of these one by one, and how you should tackle them.

Eliminate Obvious Problems

Let's eliminate some of the common things that may be a stumbling block for some people.

One thing you may want to think about is your outfit. You need to appear professional.

Though young hip kids give pitches in ripped jeans and a tea-shirt, this is one time that wearing something a little nicer may be required. If you have a button down shirt, dress pants and nice shoes, that works. Even better wear a beautiful suit. Watch out for looking un-kept or disheveled. Get a haircut or get yourself a little more organized looking. You don't have to be perfect, but looking nice will improve your chances. Yes, there are tech companies that have guys dressing in shorts every day, but that day is not this one. It shows how serious you are about this pitch.

You can completely ignore me on this, but you are what you dress in this case, especially for people seeing you for the first time. Eliminate the possibility of them thinking you are not professional or serious.

Another issue is eating correctly the day of the event. If you are starving during the event food will be on your mind. Don't leave this to chance. I always make sure I am not hungry during a pitch, because it will distract me and that ultimately will impact the investor watching you. I eat prior, even if they have food!

Other issues to eliminate are having bulky things in your pockets, which tech guys often have. Turn off your phone and other gadgets. For some reason I can't seem to keep the little dings of text messages emanating from my cell phone, even though I have turned down the volume! If you are giving a pitch, just plain outright switch the phone off, unless you need to show the cell phone app as a prop.

Eliminate what are obvious distractions and you will succeed at the focus level you require for this endeavor. You need to be smart about this. Even things like blowing your nose, taking a bathroom break, washing up before can eliminate distractions.

Now that you have removed not so important obstacles, you will be ready for your pitch.

Losing Your Mind

Let's start with this obvious problem. What happens to me in some of these pitches is I start to lose my train of thought. Why this happens to some of us, who knows. It is important to acknowledge it and then have a solution ready when it happens.

Let's say you are talking up a storm and you hit a point where you forget where you are. One simple answer for me is to keep a piece of paper around in case I lose my place. Just looking over this paper and seeing where I am in the pitch or my critical targets, gets me started again. If you are good at this and don't need to hold on to a piece of paper, that's great. However, even the best speakers lose their minds and forget where they are especially if something totally unexpected happens.

I once had a fire alarm go off in the middle of a talk and then had to continue 20 minutes later, where I left off. Most people can use their mind to go back over the critical targets and realize where they are and start again. What I recommend is a short pause. Taking a short pause for a second to think about what you need to accomplish next is fine. Actually many people listening to your pitch won't even notice you took a pause.

Don't Focus Only On Tech

Techies like myself end up focusing on the coolest part of the venture. If you get fixated on explaining small details of the features of the product you will not only not have time to discuss the business issues, you will show the investor that you have not thought through the business overall. This is probably not totally true, but don't become the person who goes on and on about the technology, overselling it! Usually savvy investors get the technology right away. At least they should be getting it right away. If they have questions about the technology they will ask you later on.

The product or service may be of critical importance. That is why you need to go over it immediately at the beginning of a pitch. But there is a limit to how far you should go. In fact, if you can explain it simply in one sentence that is understandable, that is the best way to get it done. There may be important features that either differentiate you or show a direction for the financial success. That is where the tech ends.

Don't Waste Time On Something Not Critical

You can end up finding yourself drawn to either something technical or even a marketing issue that you are passionate about.

A good example would be solving the problem. Let's say the problem you are solving is coming up with a new way to fight speeding tickets. And let's say the speed ticket app is a good solution. Once you tell an audience what the problem is and how the product solves this problem, you don't have to go into each of the small details of either how you hate cops, why you need to speed, why you will be getting back at the system or anything that is not pertinent to the business. If this happens to you, get back on track as quickly as possible.

Try to eliminate any emotional, political or other issue that shows you are a bit off. You can have passion in your start-up pitch, but leave real passion for your significant other.

Don't Forget To Mention Your Shtick

There are many cases where the entrepreneur has an important point to make, yet leave this out of their pitch. For some reason, the entrepreneur does not realize how relevant the point is to the conversation. It may have been a small detail in their head, but a big one to investors.

In one case, where the entrepreneur had an overwhelmingly important issue to let the audience know, he failed to mention that he had worked at NASA as an engineer before starting this venture. Not that this is that important, but the problem was much bigger.

His product was a physical product that he was pitching. While the product was an ok product in an ok market, he failed to mention the product had a long term opportunity to be used in outer space! Got your attention there, right!

If you are an investor, this is important stuff.

Correcting The Shtick Issue

So how do you figure out some inane part of you or your venture history that you need to expound on? Well, you need to talk with people and tell them about your venture. This goes way beyond your pitch.

You need to have somebody who either knows you well, knows your service and is somewhat an outsider find this hidden gem. Ask them, what stands out about me, my venture, my market or anything related to the pitch that investors would find either fascinating or an item that would sway them in one direction or another.

A famous professor, assistant dean, from MIT made over 112 start-up investments. Most were a dud. A few made millions, but even more important, one or two made billions. His number one criteria was they attended MIT!

Don't Lose Your Mind A Second Time

The reason I mention losing your mind a second time, is attendees of our pitch training class did not exactly listen to us! We attempted to help correct the minor and major issues in their pitches. In the end they lost their minds and reverted almost every time. Luckily we were there to ask them a question to get them back on track to their critical targets and their shticks.

You Can Not Rely On Third Parties!

It is important the founder or founders of the venture give the pitch themselves. Don't use a proxy. It never works.

So, if you are the founder and want to raise capital and you are not good at pitching, the answer is get better. Read this book. Read a bunch of other great books. Get even better at pitching. You cannot rely on a third party if they are not really at least your partner.

You need to stop losing your mind, have your paper or other tools to keep you on track. Being an expert on your subject will help keep you calm. Being an expert will get you ready to face this elevator pitch with a renewed confidence.

What is area is your personal weakness?:
Writing, Ttech, marketing, business, contracts? How are you overcoming this problem?

_____

_____

_____

_____

Are you tech only focused and not covering business issues?

_____

_____

_____

Are you relying on a prop or video? Can you skip it?

_____

_____

BE SMART, DARING & DIFFERENT. SELL A BENEFIT!

RON KLEIN

Following Up With Investors

Let's talk about the do's and don'ts of following up with potential investors. Before this conversation, it is important to discuss being prepared to follow up.

Are you prepared? Do you have an executive summary? Do you have a ten to twelve page pitch deck in PDF you can send off to the investor tomorrow as they ask for more info.

The executive summary and the pitch deck are the key points here. In rare cases the investor will want a full business plan and pro forma spreadsheets.

These words should not come as a surprise to you.

You are the prepared tech start-up giving a pitch. You know now that if you have gathered interest that the follow-up will require you to send over or drop-box these documents.

So where to start?

First off, start with common courtesy and etiquette. When the start-up pitch ends, you will find you are somewhat off. This means you probably need a drink of water or a dirty martini. I find I am on adrenaline at that point in time, and I can be a little incoherent.

The best case scenario is the investor, angel or VC approaches you and asks you a few more questions about the venture.

They will want to know some more details like how far along are you? Is this a real product yet? Is it live? Are you making revenue yet? They may want to know more about the management, the partners, who are the existing investors, if any.

Inevitably the conversation should end with "contact me" and they give you their card. More specifically you may get a question about what they need next to consider you.

You are best off by contacting the investor with a simple piece of email communications the next day or that evening about how nice it was to meet them and if there is anything else they need. This is all about the investor at this point, not about you.

If you already have the investor asking for an executive summary or your pitch deck, that is exactly what you need to send him.

If you just have a business card and they have indicated interest, then ask the investor what they need from you or if it would be ok to send him an executive summary. It is that simple.

What To Do If You Don't Have An Executive Summary

If you are asked for an executive summary, you darn better get one together as soon as possible. Good news is the executive summary is relatively easy to put together if you are a good writer.

Well, turns out most tech start-up people are not great writers. I think this is not that critical as long as the summary covers the main point.

This short book is about start-up elevator pitches not about putting together an executive summary. I am planning on writing a short book on how to write an executive summary. However, you can easily play a bunch of Youtube videos explaining how to create one. So, it is basically the same thing as your elevator pitch except with a few more details.

Executive summaries can be a few paragraphs, but typically they are one page. That is the sweet spot. I would try to stay away from two or three pages. I would also cut out anything unnecessary in the summary. It is a summary only.

The Pitch Deck

If an investor asks for your pitch deck and you do not have one, then you will be up all night. Good news is there are 100 top pitch decks out there on the web to mimic. There are even a couple of programs that will generate them for you.

I am planning on writing another short book on putting together pitch decks.

The words you will hear out there about pitch decks are 30-20-10. This means 30 size font, 20 minutes and ten pages only. It is not a rule, but it reminds us that the pitch deck in essence is a summary that allows investors to quickly figure out if this is a potential investment for them or their firm.

I have had one Silicon Valley venture capitalist tell me that the production quality of pitch decks has reached Hollywood levels. You don't have to be that extreme, you need to be professional enough not to stand out as a guy from 1999.

For instance, I have noticed that most pitch decks are no longer use bullet points. I have also noticed that great pitch decks use images and diagrams like the ones that Diane Duarte recommends in her fabulous books on presentation skills.

All of this is great and wonderful and worth your time to research, but most important is having it ready to go.

Leadership And Timeliness

When you are prepared it reflects your level of seriousness and your good character. An investor who hears from you right away knows you are ready to work with them. Having these items easily accessible makes it possible for investors to quickly engage with you.

You need to be ready for sending additional info and having your act together. The elevator pitch is just the tip of the iceberg in the path to raising capital. It is just a small item that is in front of a bunch of documents you need to have in order to show investors you know what you are doing.

How do you figure out all of these things? This is one of the great advances of the Silicon Valley community. Most other tech communities like South Florida, which I refer to as "Retirement Valley" do not have this legacy on which to rely. We can, however, learn and read up on what is current. We can find out what is required of start-ups and use this information to figure out how to be prepared. You can be anywhere in the world today creating a start-up and prepare yourself using the internet. The information is at your fingertips.

Make a list of potential investors in excel with contact info.

_____

_____

_____

_____

What nice stuff can you add to the beginning of the email when you contact the investors?

_____

_____

_____

_____

Your Checklist

The following is a checklist of all the activities you needed to have completed before your pitch and a few other important questions thrown in for good luck!

☐ Have you completed your pitch deck?

☐ What is your business name?

☐ What is your product or service name?

☐ Have you completed your executive summary?

☐ Are you prepared to say your critical targets?

☐ What is your opening line?

☐ Have you practiced your pitch with associates?

☐ Can you answer the toughest questions?

☐ Do you know your market size?

☐ Do you know how you are going to market?

- ☐ Do you know the competitors?

- ☐ What makes your business different?

- ☐ What are you looking for?

- ☐ Who is on your management team?

- ☐ Who is your board of directors?

- ☐ Describe Your Customer?

- ☐ When is your product or service going to be ready for market?

- ☐ What milestones have you accomplished?

- ☐ How much do you need monthly (your run rate) to continue this venture?

- ☐ How much have you already spent?

- ☐ Who is the CEO?

- ☐ What makes you uniquely special to start this venture at this time?

- ☐ Why this venture now?

- ☐ What is different about this venture vs. competitors?

- ☐ When did you originally start the venture? What other potential markets can the technology serve?

- ☐ What is the exit strategy, if any?

- ☐ What are you offering in terms of equity? What is the business valuation?

- ☐ Have you eaten before leaving for the venue and where you are going to pitch?

- ☐ Are you dressed appropriately?

- ☐ Do you have the directions the pitch?

- ☐ Are you sure about the pitch format, i.e. 3 min, 1 min, 10 min or speed dating format?

Notes

The following pages were added to allow you write additional notes in this book and keep those notes with you during the pitch. Also, it's a place to write down your thoughts and help prepare for the pitch!

_____

_____

_____

_____

_____

_____

_____

_____

A Few Final Words

This book was written based on a variety of tech start-up pitch events I ran in 2014 and 2015 in South Florida. The end result was that many tech start-ups need help when pitching their venture.

The first book I wrote was called *Thinking Like A Start-Up*. You can find it on Amazon.com in print or in a Kindle version. That book was based on my blog entries from 2009 to 2014. That book gave me the inspiration to write this book and the series.

The typical technology person is either not ready to pitch because they don't have their pitch organized properly or in certain cases there is a language barrier. Either way, I found there was a need for training sessions for companies pitching at our tech start-up pitch events. While teaching one of these training sessions I found the inspiration to write this book.

I did not want to write a 400 page book, because most tech start-ups need this short book and not a complete guide. They are getting ready to give a pitch tonight! So, that's why this book is so short.

This book is the first in a series I am calling **Tools For Tech Start-Ups**. Please buy each one as you need them.

Good Luck!

Quoted People

Who is Bert Decker? Bert wrote *You Have To Be Believed To Be Heard*. This book is a great starter book to learn how to be a believable speaker.

Who Is John Kemp? John, a good friend of mine has the distinction of being the rare Scottish African American as he puts it. He has been a citizen of Great Britain, South Africa and the United States. John founded both CompuStaff and Skillsoft, multi-million dollar IT job placement firms. John is currently the founder of Ecannex, a marijuana commodity exchange.

Who is Jack Karabees? Jack is a member of several active angel investment groups in South Florida as well as a speaker on start-ups and raising capital.

Who is Ron Klein? Ron was inventor of the modern credit card strip, the MLS real estate system and managing technology behind the NYSE.

Who is Duba Leibell? An active screenwriter and writing professor at the University of Miami in South Florida. Her specialty, outside of a spec script, like Miss Havana, has been story development.

Your Reading List

Through this book and my first book I mention some of my favorite start-up related books. This is your reading list. If you are a tech start-up and have not read these book, you need to start now!

Get Real: The Smarter, Faster, Easier Way to Build a Successful Web Application by Jason Fried, David Heinemeier Hansson and Matthew Linderman
Rework by Jason Fried, David Heinemeier Hansson
The Art of The Start by Guy Kawasaki
Reality Check by Guy Kawasaki
Rules For Revolutionaries by Guy Kawasaki
Don't Make Me Think by Steve Krug
Do More, Faster by Brad Feld
World Famous by David Tyreman
The Wisdom Of Crowds by James Surowiecki
What the Dog Saw, *Outliers* by Malcom Gladwell
The Launch Pad by Randall Stross
The Lean Startup by Eric Ries
All Marketers Are Liars by Seth Godin
Wikinomics by Don Tapscott and Anthony D. Williams
Getting Into Your Customer's Head by Kevin Davis
SLIDE:OLOGY by Diane Duarte
Resonate by Diane Duarte
You Got To Believed To Be Heard by Bert Decker
Inevitable Surprises by Peter Schwartz

About The Author

Though Dan Gudema aspired to be a writer as a kid, he was never able to fulfill that journey up till recently.

He has worked as a software developer, corporate manager, entrepreneur and consultant. He is a fixture in the tech Start-Up community in South Florida.

Dan has worked as an IT and Web manager or consultant for a variety of corporations like Bell Atlantic Mobile, abc Distributing, Office Depot, The Limited and NTT/Verio Inc.

Dan has several patents and this is his 2nd book about startups. In 2001 Dan co-founded and developed as a programmer Pre-Dating Speed Dating, which became the largest speed dating company in the US. It was sold to Cupid.com in 2004.

Originally from Parsippany, NJ, Dan moved to South Florida in 1997. He attended the University of Maryland for his BA and has an MBA from Florida Atlantic University. In 2004, Dan won a business plan contest at Florida Atlantic University while in their MBA program. Since 2014 he has run StartupPOP pitch events. You can learn more about Dan at StartupPOP.com.

Please visit either Amazon.com or Gumroad.com to buy my other books.

www.ingramcontent.com/pod-product-compliance
Lightning Source LLC
Chambersburg PA
CBHW020919180526
45163CB00007B/2805